Please write what effort you put in today for your "team", the people
you meet face-to-face on a regular basis in your day-to-day life.

Please write what effort you put in today for your "team", the people

you meet face-to-face on a regular basis in your day-to-day life.

Please write what effort you put in today for your "team", the people
you meet face-to-face on a regular basis in your day-to-day life.

Please write what effort you put in today for your "team", the people
you meet face-to-face on a regular basis in your day-to-day life.

Please write what effort you put in today for your "team", the people

you meet face-to-face on a regular basis in your day-to-day life.

Please write what effort you put in today for your "team", the people you meet face-to-face on a regular basis in your day-to-day life.

Please write what effort you put in today for your "team", the people
you meet face-to-face on a regular basis in your day-to-day life.

Please write what effort you put in today for your "team", the people

you meet face-to-face on a regular basis in your day-to-day life.

Please write what effort you put in today for your "team", the people
you meet face-to-face on a regular basis in your day-to-day life.

Please write what effort you put in today for your "team", the people
you meet face-to-face on a regular basis in your day-to-day life.

Please write what effort you put in today for your "team", the people

you meet face-to-face on a regular basis in your day-to-day life.

Please write what effort you put in today for your "team", the people
you meet face-to-face on a regular basis in your day-to-day life.

Please write what effort you put in today for your "team", the people
you meet face-to-face on a regular basis in your day-to-day life.

Please write what effort you put in today for your "team", the people

you meet face-to-face on a regular basis in your day-to-day life.

Please write what effort you put in today for your "team", the people
you meet face-to-face on a regular basis in your day-to-day life.

Please write what effort you put in today for your "team", the people
you meet face-to-face on a regular basis in your day-to-day life.

Please write what effort you put in today for your "team", the people
you meet face-to-face on a regular basis in your day-to-day life.

Please write what effort you put in today for your "team", the people
you meet face-to-face on a regular basis in your day-to-day life.

Please write what effort you put in today for your "team", the people
you meet face-to-face on a regular basis in your day-to-day life.

Please write what effort you put in today for your "team", the people
you meet face-to-face on a regular basis in your day-to-day life.

Please write what effort you put in today for your "team", the people
you meet face-to-face on a regular basis in your day-to-day life.

Please write what effort you put in today for your "team", the people

you meet face-to-face on a regular basis in your day-to-day life.

Please write what effort you put in today for your "team", the people
you meet face-to-face on a regular basis in your day-to-day life.

Please write what effort you put in today for your "team", the people
you meet face-to-face on a regular basis in your day-to-day life.

Please write what effort you put in today for your "team", the people

you meet face-to-face on a regular basis in your day-to-day life.

Please write what effort you put in today for your "team", the people
you meet face-to-face on a regular basis in your day-to-day life.

Please write what effort you put in today for your "team", the people
you meet face-to-face on a regular basis in your day-to-day life.

Please write what effort you put in today for your "team", the people

you meet face-to-face on a regular basis in your day-to-day life.

Please write what effort you put in today for your "team", the people you meet face-to-face on a regular basis in your day-to-day life.

Please write what effort you put in today for your "team", the people
you meet face-to-face on a regular basis in your day-to-day life.

Please write what effort you put in today for your "team", the people
you meet face-to-face on a regular basis in your day-to-day life.

Please write what effort you put in today for your "team", the people
you meet face-to-face on a regular basis in your day-to-day life.

Please write what effort you put in today for your "team", the people
    you meet face-to-face on a regular basis in your day-to-day life.

Please write what effort you put in today for your "team", the people

you meet face-to-face on a regular basis in your day-to-day life.

Please write what effort you put in today for your "team", the people
you meet face-to-face on a regular basis in your day-to-day life.

Please write what effort you put in today for your "team", the people
you meet face-to-face on a regular basis in your day-to-day life.

Please write what effort you put in today for your "team", the people

you meet face-to-face on a regular basis in your day-to-day life.

Please write what effort you put in today for your "team", the people
you meet face-to-face on a regular basis in your day-to-day life.

Please write what effort you put in today for your "team", the people
you meet face-to-face on a regular basis in your day-to-day life.

Please write what effort you put in today for your "team", the people
you meet face-to-face on a regular basis in your day-to-day life.

Please write what effort you put in today for your "team", the people
you meet face-to-face on a regular basis in your day-to-day life.

Please write what effort you put in today for your "team", the people

you meet face-to-face on a regular basis in your day-to-day life.

Please write what effort you put in today for your "team", the people
you meet face-to-face on a regular basis in your day-to-day life.

Please write what effort you put in today for your "team", the people
you meet face-to-face on a regular basis in your day-to-day life.

Please write what effort you put in today for your "team", the people

you meet face-to-face on a regular basis in your day-to-day life.

Please write what effort you put in today for your "team", the people
you meet face-to-face on a regular basis in your day-to-day life.

Please write what effort you put in today for your "team", the people
you meet face-to-face on a regular basis in your day-to-day life.

Please write what effort you put in today for your "team", the people

you meet face-to-face on a regular basis in your day-to-day life.

Please write what effort you put in today for your "team", the people
you meet face-to-face on a regular basis in your day-to-day life.

Please write what effort you put in today for your "team", the people
you meet face-to-face on a regular basis in your day-to-day life.

Please write what effort you put in today for your "team", the people

you meet face-to-face on a regular basis in your day-to-day life.

Please write what effort you put in today for your "team", the people
you meet face-to-face on a regular basis in your day-to-day life.

Please write what effort you put in today for your "team", the people
you meet face-to-face on a regular basis in your day-to-day life.

Please write what effort you put in today for your "team", the people

you meet face-to-face on a regular basis in your day-to-day life.

Please write what effort you put in today for your "team", the people
you meet face-to-face on a regular basis in your day-to-day life.

Please write what effort you put in today for your "team", the people
you meet face-to-face on a regular basis in your day-to-day life.

Please write what effort you put in today for your "team", the people
you meet face-to-face on a regular basis in your day-to-day life.

Please write what effort you put in today for your "team", the people
you meet face-to-face on a regular basis in your day-to-day life.

Please write what effort you put in today for your "team", the people
you meet face-to-face on a regular basis in your day-to-day life.

Please write what effort you put in today for your "team", the people
you meet face-to-face on a regular basis in your day-to-day life.

Printed in Great Britain
by Amazon